Magical Mix-Ups

Friends and Fashion

Look out
for other
Magical
Mix-Ups!

Magical Mix-Ups
Birthdays and Bridesmaids

Magical Mix-Ups: Friends and Fashion
Published in the UK in 2012 by Nosy Crow Ltd
The Crow's Nest, 10a Lant Street
London SE1 1QR

www. nosycrow.com

Nosy Crow and associated logos are trademarks and/or registered trademarks of Nosy Crow Ltd

Text copyright © Marnie Edwards 2012
Illustrations copyright © Leigh Hodgkinson 2012

The right of Marnie Edwards to be identified as the author
and Leigh Hodgkinson to be identified as the illustrator of this work has been asserted.

A CIP catalogue record for this book is available from the British Library

ISBN: 978 0 85763 122 0

Printed in China

1 3 5 7 9 8 6 4 2

Magical Mix-Ups

Friends and Fashion

Marnie Edwards * Leigh Hodgkinson

nosy crow

Who's Who in MIXTOPIA

Emerald the Witch

Princess Sapphire

Boris – Emerald's toad

You'll need these . . .

Drawing
- - - - -
TOOLS

Using different tools helps
create great drawings

PENCIL

COLOURED PENCIL

CRAYON

Decorating TOOLS

Stick these in to add extra SPARKLE and MAGIC

Sequins

Pencil rubbings

Silver foil

Glitter

Drawing Tips

Turn to the back of the book for drawing and design ideas!

Chapter 1

The **BEST** OF friends

Add doors
and windows
to the castle

Who is playing by the fountains?

Where does
this path go?

Add patterned hills
in the background

Draw wonky
stepping stones
up to Emerald's
house

Princess Sapphire and Emerald the Witch are
best friends. They live next door to each other
in Mixtopia, a land where anything can happen,
and usually does.

Sapphire loves
clothes, shoes
and looking neat.

Draw
Sapphire's
perfect
hair

Clothes

Shoes

Emerald loves her pet toad, Boris, and can't remember if she owns a hairbrush.

Draw Emerald's messy hair

What do you think?

HAIRBRUSH?
YES ☐
NO ☑

Colour in Emerald's witchy outfit

They may be very different, but both girls love books, magazines and comics!

Draw Boris up to no good!

Think of a funny title for this book!

CROWNS & SPARKLE

how to make YOUR crown shimmer & SPARKLE

FREE GIFT

TOADSTOOLS & TIARAS

What is the free gift?

Add more magazines to the pile

Design the magazine's cover

Sapphire's favourite magazine is *Kind Hearts and Coronets*. "Ooh, a quiz!" she cries.

Fill in the princess quiz

Kind Hearts and Coronets

Which Princess are You?

Do you like:

A) sparkly glittery things?

B) stroking slugs?

Do you live in:

A) a castle?

B) a spaceship?

Do you wear:

(A) a tiara? ☐

(B) flippers? ☐

Do you:

(A) giggle and squeal a lot? ☑

(B) burp and sniff a lot? ☐

Number of (A)s

4

Number of (B)s

0

If you had mostly (A)s you are a very good princess.

If you had mostly (B)s you are a rubbish princess.

Draw a very good princess here

Draw a rubbish princess here

Emerald and her toad, Boris, are reading *Wizard & Chips*. It's their favourite magazine.

Fill in this comic strip

Then Boris sneezes loudly. "Bless you," says Emerald.

Boris is just blowing
his nose when Sapphire
suddenly squeaks
with excitement.
"Look at this, Em!"
she cries, waving
her magazine
around madly.

Colour in Sapphire's hair and crown

Draw
Sapphire's
excited face

ATTENTION

all you crafty princesses!

Empress maisie

needs an outfit for her

BIRTHDAY PARTY

and she needs **YOU** to make it for her.

The winning outfit will be chosen at a

FANTABULOUS

Fashion Show at the

GRAND Palace

in **2** days' time!

Ready, steady – sew!

Design the magazine border!

Princess Sapphire's eyes are shining.
"I can't wait to get started!" she says.
Suddenly, Boris sneezes so hard he
topples off Emerald's shoulder!
Boris the Toad is not well . . .

Colour in
Sapphire

Finish the tumble line

Draw a
box of tissues
for Boris

Chapter 2

Buttons and Bobbins

Poor Boris has taken to his bed. "Time for a get-well potion," thinks Emerald. "I'll need some things . . ." She makes a shopping list and sets off for the shops.

What is on TV?

Add more zapps

ICE CREAM

What flavour is the ice cream? Colour it in.

Draw her shopping basket

Draw Emerald's broomstick by the door

Put on Emerald's cloak

Meanwhile, Sapphire is rummaging through the Royal Scrap Box. There are loads of lovely things she can use for Empress Maisie's outfit in there . . .

Off flies Emerald!

Design pretty patterns on the fabric scraps

Add
more piles
of buttons

Stick in
your button
rubbings

What is Sapphire holding?

Decorate the side of the button box

Sapphire then heads off to find the Royal Button Box. What a treasure trove!

"Now, what would little Maisie like to wear?" she thinks.

She looks at the magazine again and spots some tiny writing she missed before.

Things **YOU** should **KNOW**
Empress Maisie **LiKES** **butterflies**, **DANCING** and **tRAMPOLINING** She **HATES** scratchy labels and corduroy. She's not great at tying shoelaces.

Doodle more butterflies

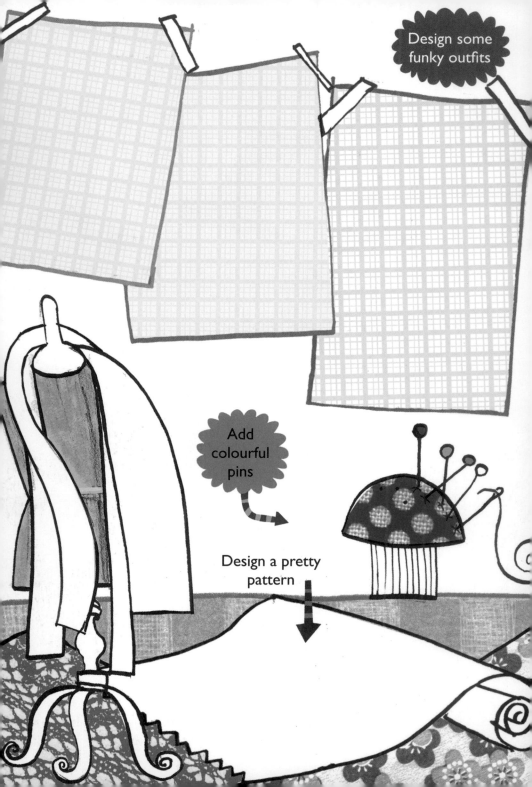

Design some funky outfits

Add colourful pins

Design a pretty pattern

"A-ha!" cries Princess Sapphire, settling herself at her work table. "I've got the perfect idea!"

As Sapphire gets to work, poorly Boris sighs in his sleep and turns over . . .

Chapter 3

A
FLYING
visit

As she flies over Shopping City, Emerald sees a big department store. "*Spellfridges!*" she thinks. "Perfect." She points her broomstick towards the landing pad on its roof, and joins the queue of witches circling in the sky.

Finish her line of flight

Add more chimneys and swirly smoke

Add more witches waiting to land

Design a fancy *Spellfridges* sign

Emerald looks at the ingredients she needs for Boris's get-well potion. They're mostly disgusting. "Rather you than me, Boris," she says.

Draw some of the ingredients

Stuff for
BORIS

peaches in ~~toffee~~
CHOCOLATE sauce

toenail clippings (& HAIR)

12 magic beans

1 drop of MAGIC
POTION no 83
(* handle with CARE!)

SQUID INK (purple)

2 jelly stars

WITCHETTY gruBs
& honeY AntS

What else would a witch buy from the shops?

GENERAL Stuff

Draw your made-up stuff

First, Emerald heads for the deli counter.
Her mouth waters – what amazing delicacies!

Add more jars and bottles to the shelves

Fill the trays with goodies

jelly stars

deep fried snails

magic beans

THE MAGIC deli

She might just treat herself to a deep-fried snail or two, even if they will spoil her lunch.

What is reflected in the mirrors?

Draw a fancy frame

"My, these snails are chewy," thinks Emerald as she goes into the Beauty Room.

Next, Emerald excitedly pushes open the door to the *Lotions & Potions* room. Everything sparkles and shines, and the witch behind the counter has AMAZING hair!

Add more bows

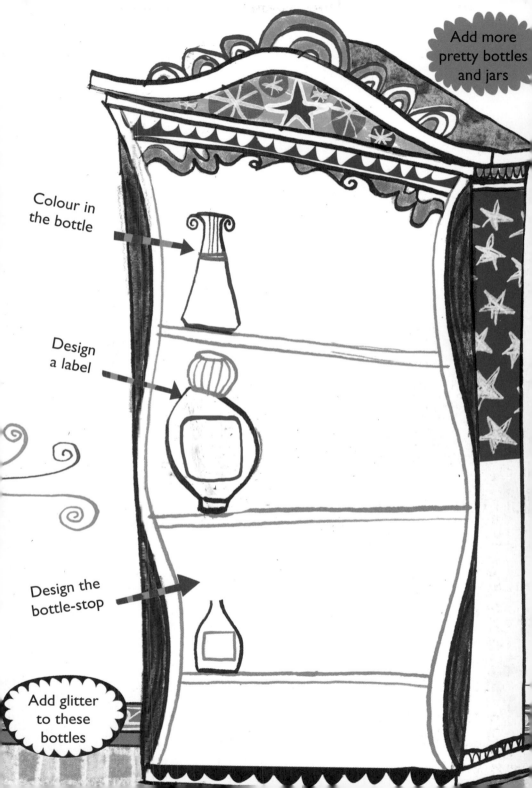

Add more pretty bottles and jars

Colour in the bottle

Design a label

Design the bottle-stop

Add glitter to these bottles

Back at home, Emerald takes everything she has bought into her laboratory. "Bubble, bubble, boil and, er…" she says. "Oh, I can never remember how that goes!"

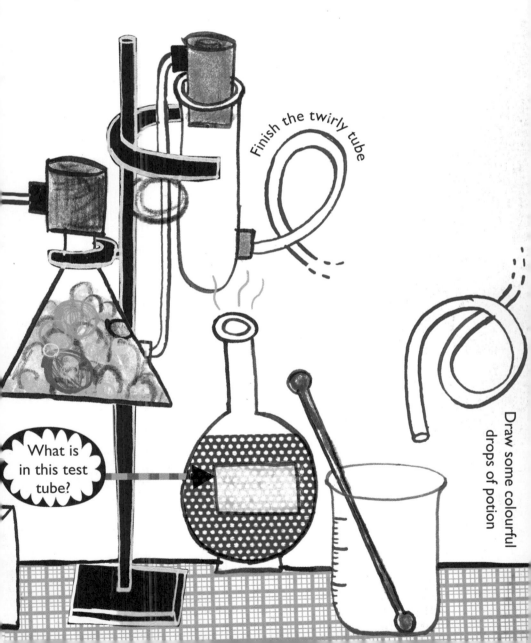

One small explosion later, the get-well potion is ready! Emerald carefully takes it to Boris, who doesn't look very pleased to see her, or the big spoon . . .

What is Boris thinking?

Draw a big, dripping spoon of medicine

Chapter 4

UP, UP and AWAY

Are there stars in the sky?

Has Sapphire got a bedtime drink?

Design a funky duvet cover for Sapphire

Night is falling and, at the castle, Princess Sapphire is getting ready for bed. She has pricked her fingers with her needle so many times she feels just like Sleeping Beauty!

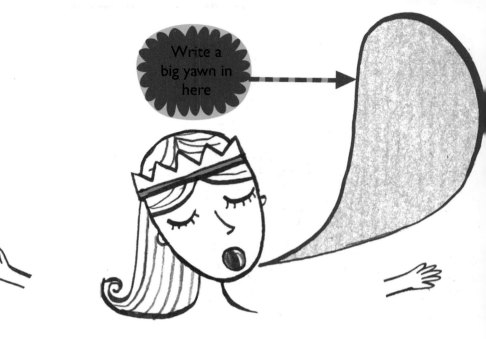

Write a
big yawn in
here

Design some
princess
pyjamas

Sapphire is woken up bright and early by Emerald landing on her carpet. "I do wish you'd use the door occasionally," she grumbles.

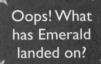

But her friend isn't listening. "Boris is better!" Emerald cries happily. But just then, Boris gives an ENORMOUS sneeze. "Well, almost better," she adds.

"We've come to help you," says Emerald. "We've got some BRILLIANT ideas for Maisie's outfit…"

What outfit would <u>YOU</u> make?

"But I've finished!" says Sapphire, pointing to her dressmaker's dummy. "Look!"

Who is sitting on the pincushion?

It's time to leave for the Grand Palace. The Royal Hot-Air Balloon is ready and waiting on the lawn, and Boris is wearing his best scarf.

Add more cute creatures

Add trees and flowers on the hills

Who is flying in the sky?

Design a patchwork balloon pattern using fabric, paper and wrappers to make a collage

Add flames

Do some pencil rubbings to add texture to the basket

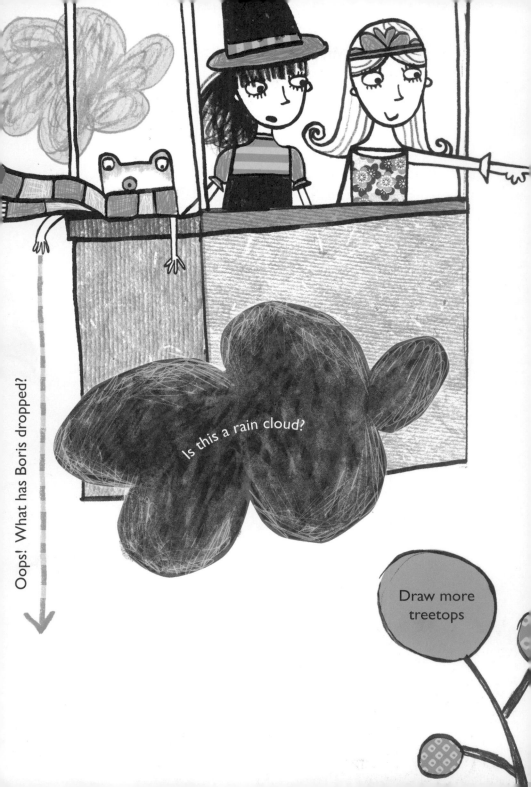

Soon they are high in the sky.
"Mind those flying ponies!" says Sapphire.
"They look a bit wobbly," worries Emerald.

Draw more flying ponies

Look!
A rainbow!

Just then, they spy Empress Maisie's Grand Palace down below. It's almost time for the Fashion Show!

Use pencil rubbings to decorate the Grand Palace

Colour in the flag and draw some trees

Chapter 5

M O D E L

Behaviour

The balloon lands gently on the palace lawn.

Why is Empress Maisie looking grumpy?

Reason 1

Reason 2

Reason 3

Empress Maisie is waiting to greet them. She looks a bit grumpy. Maybe it's because her jumper is SO scratchy and her belt is too tight?

Add more Royal Bunting

What does the sign say?

The Fashion Show will take place in a huge marquee.
Inside, everyone is rushing about getting things ready.

Add more Royal Bunting

Draw more grand flower displays in the vases

Princess Sapphire peeps into the dressing room and gasps. Ooh la la, the glamour!

Draw the models' reflections in the mirrors

Draw the missing shoes to make pairs

What else is on the dressing table?

A girl with very long hair comes over.
"Hello," she says. "I'm Poppy.
That's my outfit over there."

POPPY's outfit

ENTRY NUMBER

1

Where is Boris hiding?

Finish colouring in Poppy's outfit

Add more colourful ribbons

What shoes would you put with Poppy's outfit?

"And that's mine next to it,"
says another girl, pointing.
"My name's Lulu. I love your toad!"
Boris beams with pleasure, before
giving a HUGE sneeze.

Decorate
Sapphire's
skirt

Sapphire introduces herself nervously . . . .

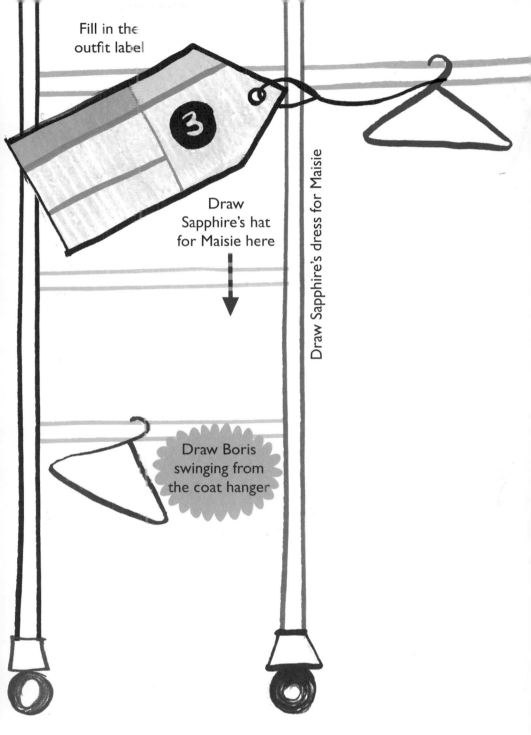

Fill in the outfit label

3

Draw Sapphire's hat for Maisie here

Draw Sapphire's dress for Maisie

Draw Boris swinging from the coat hanger

. . . and hangs up her outfit next to the others.

But nothing could
possibly go wrong.

Could it?

Draw in possible
things that could
go wrong in each
section

Chapter 6

A Fashion FIASCO

Is she wearing dangly earrings?

Give the ladies big sunglasses

Emerald, Sapphire and Boris take their seats next to the catwalk. A lady in the row behind taps Emerald on the shoulder with her long, red nail. "I can't see," she complains. "Please put your hat on the floor!"

Emerald looks but there is nowhere to put her hat.

Emerald decides to take her hat to the dressing room. As she opens the door, Boris sneezes so mightly that he flies off Emerald's shoulder again and knocks all the outfits into a muddle on the floor.

Emerald tries to put them back together again but she is not sure she has got it right . . .

Add
more
musical
notes

Draw a swooshy curtain

What is Boris
doing on the
catwalk?

Draw in the models' hair

Sapphire, Poppy and Lulu stare at the models in horror. All the outfits are muddled up!

But then the crowd starts clapping and stamping their feet in delight. The outfits are a huge hit!

Oops! Where is the tiny dog?

What do the crowd throw in the air?

Give Poppy and Lulu bunches of flowers too

"They're brilliant – all of them," exclaims Empress Maisie. "Now I have three birthday outfits instead of one!"

She is so happy that she throws a special trampolining party to celebrate!

Add more yummy things to the picnic

Draw everyone's shoes lined up here

Draw bouncy boing lines

Who else is bouncing on the trampoline?

"I'm sorry I mixed everything up," says Emerald to Sapphire as they head home in the Royal Hot-Air Balloon.

Look! Poppy is riding home on a magic bicycle

Look! Lulu is riding a flying pony

Can you add silver foil tiny stars?

Draw the turrets of the Grand Palace down below

"That's all right," says Sapphire, and she gives her best friend a big hug. "But remind me never to ask you for any fashion tips!"

The Big Picture
Draw your favourite moments from the book, and stick in your favourite things

picture GLOSSARY

If you need a helping hand thinking of things to draw then check these ideas out!

Royal Fish

Sneeze Effect

ATcHOOO!

Other things Maisie doesn't like

What's on TV?

WITCH FACTOR

Stars

Creatures

Magic Beans

Flying Witch

Boris's Dream

Magic Bicycle

Sapphire's Bedtime Drink

Trees

KING BORIS

Flowers